FROM THE GRILL OF...

THIS BOOK BELONGS TO:

....

....

GIVEN BY:

....

....

OCCASION:

....

....

TABLE OF CONTENTS

INTRODUCTION

THE FIVE-INGREDIENT REVOLUTION

Welcome to *The 5-Ingredient BBQ Cookbook for Men* — the only cookbook you'll ever need when the grill's hot, the fridge is half-empty, and your stomach's making decisions faster than your brain.

This isn't a chef's manual filled with fussy steps, hard-to-find spices, or thirty-dollar marinades. This is the playbook for **real men who love bold flavor, cold drinks, and fire that bites back.**
You'll find over 50 recipes that prove simplicity doesn't mean boring — it means **mastery through minimalism.** With just five ingredients, you'll be making ribs that rival restaurants, steaks that silence the table, and wings that disappear before you sit down.

Whether you're:

- **Grilling for the guys on game night,**

- **Cooking up a quick family dinner,** or

- **Trying to impress someone who doesn't yet believe you can cook,**

...this book's got you covered.
Every recipe is built for speed, taste, and victory — with easy-to-follow steps, nutrition facts, and space to jot down your own twists.

So pour yourself a cold one, fire up the grill, and remember: this isn't just cooking — it's a ritual.

MAN RULES OF THE GRILL

Because barbecue isn't a recipe... it's a code.

Rule #1: Don't apologize for the smoke. That's flavor in the air.
Rule #2: The guy holding the tongs is in charge — no exceptions.
Rule #3: Flip once. Stare proudly. Sip beer. Repeat.
Rule #4: If there's no char, you're doing it wrong.
Rule #5: Meat rests longer than your patience. Respect that.
Rule #6: Don't measure rubs. Feel them in your soul.
Rule #7: Fire solves more problems than it causes.
Rule #8: Never waste marinade — it's liquid ambition.
Rule #9: Smoke on your shirt is a badge of honor.
Rule #10: If someone asks for "medium well," tell them there's chicken.

So let's get to it — less talk, more sizzle. The coals are hot, the tongs are calling, and your next great meal starts with just five ingredients.

BEEF KINGS

GRILLED FLANK STEAK WITH CHILI BUTTER

A spicy-sweet butter that melts right into victory.

Prep: 10 min   Cook: 10 min   Serves: 3–4

YOU'LL NEED

- 1½ lb flank steak
- ¼ cup butter, softened
- 2 tbsp chili paste (sambal oelek or similar)
- 2 cloves garlic, minced
- 2 tbsp honey

Five ingredients. That's all between you and greatness.

HOW TO MAKE IT

1. **Blend** butter, chili paste, garlic, and honey until smooth; set aside.
2. **Pat dry** the flank steak and season both sides generously with salt and pepper.
3. **Grill** over medium-high heat, about 4–5 minutes per side for medium-rare.
4. **Spread** the chili butter over the hot steak as soon as it leaves the grill—let it melt into a glaze.
5. **Rest** 5–10 minutes, then slice thinly *against the grain*.

⚙ GRILL FUEL STATS (per serving)

Calories: 420 | **Protein:** 35 g | **Fat:** 26 g | **Carbs:** 7 g | **Sugar:** 6 g | **Fiber:** 0 g
Approximate values based on a 6 oz portion.

💧 Pitmaster Tip

Try a knob of chili butter on grilled corn or baked potatoes — pure smoky gold.

📑 Victory Notes

How did it turn out?

....

....

Next time I'll try it with:

....

....

"Butter and smoke — the true power couple."

5-INGREDIENT BEEF SATAY SKEWERS

Big flavor on a stick — no fuss, all fire.

Prep: 15 min   Cook: 8 min   Serves: 4

YOU'LL NEED

- 1 lb flank steak, thinly sliced (¼-inch strips)
- ¼ cup soy sauce (low sodium)
- ¼ cup balsamic vinegar
- 1 tbsp honey
- 1 tbsp minced garlic

Five ingredients, one mission — flavor domination.

HOW TO MAKE IT

1. **Whisk** soy sauce, balsamic vinegar, honey, and garlic in a bowl.
2. **Add** beef strips, coat well, and marinate 30 minutes (or overnight).
3. **Thread** meat onto skewers (soak bamboo skewers in water first).
4. **Grill** over medium-high heat for 3–4 minutes per side until browned and juicy.
5. **Rest** a couple of minutes, then serve hot — or cold straight from the fridge.

⚙ GRILL FUEL STATS (per serving)

Calories: 270 | **Protein:** 29 g | **Fat:** 12 g | **Carbs:** 7 g | **Sugar:** 6 g | **Fiber:** 0 g

Approximate values based on 4 oz beef per serving.

⬤ Pitmaster Tip

Brush the skewers with leftover marinade during the final minute for a caramelized glaze — just boil it first for safety.

▤ Victory Notes

How did it turn out?

....

....

Next time I'll try it with:

....

....

"Stick it, flip it, own it."

CLASSIC BURGER PATTIES

Five ingredients. Zero excuses. Pure backyard glory.

Prep: 10 min   Cook: 8 min   Serves: 4

YOU'LL NEED

- 2 lb ground beef (80% lean)
- 1 tsp coarse black pepper
- 1 tsp kosher salt
- 2 tbsp Dijon mustard
- 1½ tbsp Worcestershire sauce

That's all it takes to make every fast-food burger taste like regret.

HOW TO MAKE IT

1. **Mix** beef, pepper, salt, mustard, and Worcestershire in a bowl — gently, don't mash it.

2. **Form** into 4 thick patties and press a small dimple in the center of each (for even cooking).

3. **Grill** over high heat, about 3–4 minutes per side for medium. Don't press them — you're not squeezing out toothpaste.

4. **Rest** 2 minutes, then serve on toasted buns with whatever you call toppings.

⚙ GRILL FUEL STATS (per patty)

Calories: 370 | **Protein:** 31 g | **Fat:** 26 g | **Carbs:** 1 g | **Sugar:** 0 g | **Fiber:** 0 g
Approximate values for a 6-oz patty (no bun).

🜄 Pitmaster Tip

Add a cube of cold butter in the center before grilling for a juicy core that melts as you bite.

📜 Victory Notes

How did it turn out?

....

....

Next time I'll try it with:

....

....

"Respect the patty. Fear the spatula."

TERIYAKI STEAK & PINEAPPLE SKEWERS

Sweet, smoky, and dangerously easy to crush.

Prep: 15 min   Cook: 10 min   Serves: 4

YOU'LL NEED

- 1½ lb beef sirloin or ribeye, cut into 1½-inch cubes
- 2 cups pineapple chunks (fresh or canned, drained)
- 1 large bell pepper, cut into pieces
- 1 red onion, cut into chunks
- 1 cup teriyaki sauce (store-bought or homemade)

That's five. If you're counting skewers as ingredients, you're overthinking it.

HOW TO MAKE IT

1. **Marinate** the beef cubes in ½ cup teriyaki sauce for 15–30 minutes.
2. **Thread** beef, pineapple, pepper, and onion onto skewers in any pattern that says "grill god."
3. **Grill** over medium heat for about 8–10 minutes, turning and brushing with extra teriyaki sauce.
4. **Glaze** once more right before removing from heat.
5. **Rest** 3 minutes, then serve sticky, smoky, and sweet.

⚙ GRILL FUEL STATS (per serving)

Calories: 355 | **Protein:** 33 g | **Fat:** 18 g | **Carbs:** 15 g | **Sugar:** 11 g | **Fiber:** 1 g

Approximate values for ¼ of total yield.

🔥 Pitmaster Tip

Add jalapeño slices between chunks for a fiery twist — sweet heat never loses.

🗄 Victory Notes

How did it turn out?

....

....

Next time I'll try it with:

....

....

"If it drips, it's working."

BALSAMIC GLAZED STEAK KEBABS

Grill marks meet sweet glaze — no silverware needed.

Prep: 20 min   Cook: 10 min   Serves: 4

YOU'LL NEED

- 1 lb beef sirloin, cut into 1½-inch cubes
- 1 pint cherry tomatoes
- ¼ cup BBQ sauce
- ¼ cup balsamic vinegar
- 1 tbsp Dijon mustard

Five ingredients, one sticky masterpiece.

HOW TO MAKE IT

1. **Whisk** BBQ sauce, balsamic vinegar, and Dijon mustard in a small bowl.
2. **Toss** beef cubes in most of the glaze (save a few tablespoons for later) and marinate 30 minutes.
3. **Thread** beef and cherry tomatoes onto skewers — red and brown never looked so good together.
4. **Grill** over medium-high heat about 8–10 minutes, turning and basting with the reserved glaze.
5. **Rest** 3 minutes before serving. Sticky fingers encouraged.

⚙ GRILL FUEL STATS (per serving)

Calories: 320 | **Protein:** 31 g | **Fat:** 14 g | **Carbs:** 15 g | **Sugar:** 11 g |
Fiber: 1 g
Approximate values for one-quarter of total yield.

◊ Pitmaster Tip

Swap the cherry tomatoes for mushrooms if you want more umami than juice
— both soak up glaze like champs.

▤ Victory Notes

How did it turn out?

....

....

Next time I'll try it with:

....

....

"If your grill isn't messy, you're not doing it right."

SMOKED SALT-AND-PEPPER STEAK

Three ingredients. Infinite bragging rights.

Prep: 5 min   Cook: 60–90 min   Serves: 2

YOU'LL NEED

- 1 thick-cut steak (ribeye or strip, 1½–2 inches thick)
- Kosher salt, to taste
- Coarse black pepper, to taste

That's it — steak, salt, pepper, smoke, and patience.

HOW TO MAKE IT

1. **Season** the steak liberally on all sides with coarse salt and pepper.
2. **Set up** your smoker or grill for indirect low heat (around 225°F).
3. **Smoke** the steak for 60–90 minutes, or until the internal temp hits 125–130°F for medium-rare.
4. **Sear** quickly over high heat (or in a cast-iron pan) for 1 minute per side to build a crust.
5. **Rest** 5 minutes before slicing. Taste first, thank yourself later.

GRILL FUEL STATS (per serving)

Calories: 460 | **Protein:** 39 g | **Fat:** 33 g | **Carbs:** 0 g | **Sugar:** 0 g | **Fiber:** 0 g
Approximate values for an 8 oz portion of ribeye.

◐ Pitmaster Tip

For perfect crust, rest the steak 5 minutes after smoking, then hit it over roaring heat — that reverse sear is your secret weapon.

▊ Victory Notes

How did it turn out?

....

....

Next time I'll try it with:

....

....

"Three ingredients. One religion."

SANTA MARIA TRI-TIP (SPG RUB)

California's gift to the grill — simple, smoky, and sacred.

Prep: 10 min   Cook: 30–40 min   Serves: 6–8

YOU'LL NEED

- 1 tri-tip roast (2–3 lb)
- 2 tsp kosher salt
- 2 tsp freshly ground black pepper
- 1 tsp garlic powder
- (Optional) Splash of olive oil to help rub stick

Four ingredients, one legendary flavor.

HOW TO MAKE IT

1. **Pat dry** the tri-tip and coat lightly with olive oil (if using).
2. **Mix** salt, pepper, and garlic powder and rub it deep into the meat on all sides.
3. **Grill** over medium-high heat, turning every 3–4 minutes ("flip forever" method) until internal temp reaches 130–135 °F for medium-rare.
4. **Rest** 10 minutes before slicing *against the grain*.
5. **Serve** with a handshake and a cold beer — you've earned it.

⚙ GRILL FUEL STATS (per serving)

Calories: 360 | **Protein:** 37 g | **Fat:** 22 g | **Carbs:** 0 g | **Sugar:** 0 g | **Fiber:** 0 g

Approximate values for a 6 oz serving of tri-tip.

◊ Pitmaster Tip

Slice the tri-tip in two directions — each half has a different grain. Cutting it right makes all the difference between tender and tough.

▤ Victory Notes

How did it turn out?

....

....

Next time I'll try it with:

....

....

"Salt. Pepper. Garlic. Faith."

TEXAS-STYLE SMOKED BRISKET

Salt. Pepper. Smoke. Time. That's the whole religion.

Prep: 20 min   Cook: 10–12 hr   Serves: 10–12

YOU'LL NEED

- 1 whole beef brisket (packer cut, 8–12 lb)
- ½ cup kosher salt
- 1 cup coarse black pepper
- (Optional) 1 tbsp garlic powder — Texas purists will forgive you
- Wood chunks for smoking (oak or hickory preferred)

Five ingredients if you count patience — and you should.

HOW TO MAKE IT

1. **Trim** excess fat, leaving a ¼-inch fat cap on the brisket.
2. **Blend** salt and pepper into a 50/50 rub (add garlic powder if using).
3. **Coat** the brisket generously on every side.
4. **Smoke** at 225 °F for 4–5 hours until internal temp reaches about 165 °F.
5. **Wrap** tightly in butcher paper or foil and continue smoking until 195–203 °F and a probe slides in like butter.
6. **Rest** wrapped for 1 hour before slicing *against the grain*.

⚙ GRILL FUEL STATS (per serving)

Calories: 440 | **Protein:** 37 g | **Fat:** 31 g | **Carbs:** 0 g | **Sugar:** 0 g | **Fiber:** 0 g

Approximate values for a 6 oz serving of smoked brisket.

◐ Pitmaster Tip

If the bark feels soft after wrapping, unwrap and finish the last 30 minutes unwrapped to firm it up. That's where the magic happens.

▤ Victory Notes

How did it turn out?

....

....

Next time I'll try it with:

....

....

"Time + smoke = respect."

SMOKED BEEF SHORT RIBS (SALT & PEPPER)

The caveman cut. Simple. Slow. Unstoppable.

Prep: 10 min   Cook: 6 hr   Serves: 4–6

YOU'LL NEED

- 4 beef short ribs (plate or chuck cut, about 4 lb total)
- 6 tbsp coarse black pepper
- 2 tbsp kosher salt
- (Optional) 1 tbsp garlic powder for a deeper crust
- Oak or hickory wood chunks for smoking

Three ingredients, one ritual — and a smoker that smells like heaven.

HOW TO MAKE IT

1. **Trim** ribs of excess fat and silver skin if needed.
2. **Combine** pepper and salt (add garlic powder if you're not a purist).
3. **Season** the ribs liberally on all sides — they need a thick coat.
4. **Smoke** at 275 °F for 5–6 hours, or until the internal temp hits 200–205 °F and a probe slides in with no resistance.
5. **Rest** 30 minutes before slicing between bones. Serve with pride and a stack of napkins.

⚙ GRILL FUEL STATS (per serving)

Calories: 610 | **Protein:** 45 g | **Fat:** 48 g | **Carbs:** 0 g | **Sugar:** 0 g | **Fiber:** 0 g

Approximate values for one large rib portion.

🔥 Pitmaster Tip

Cook these in a foil pan for the last hour to catch rendered fat — it becomes liquid gold for brushing over slices before serving.

📓 Victory Notes

How did it turn out?

....

....

Next time I'll try it with:

....

....

"Low, slow, and loud — that's how legends cook."

POOR MAN S BURNT ENDS (CHUCK ROAST)

Brisket flavor. Half the price. All the glory.

Prep: 15 min   Cook: 5 hr   Serves: 6–8

YOU'LL NEED

- 3 lb beef chuck roast
- 2 tbsp Dijon mustard
- 3 tbsp BBQ seasoning or rub
- ½ cup barbecue sauce
- 2 tbsp brown sugar

Five ingredients that turn cheap beef into championship candy.

HOW TO MAKE IT

1. **Coat** the chuck roast with Dijon mustard, then cover with BBQ rub.
2. **Smoke** at 250 °F for 3–4 hours, until internal temp hits around 200 °F and the roast feels tender.
3. **Rest** briefly, then cut into 1-inch cubes and place in a foil pan.
4. **Toss** cubes with BBQ sauce and brown sugar until coated.
5. **Return** to the smoker (uncovered) for 45–60 minutes, stirring once, until caramelized and sticky.

⚙ GRILL FUEL STATS (per serving)

Calories: 480 | **Protein:** 37 g | **Fat:** 29 g | **Carbs:** 14 g | **Sugar:** 10 g | **Fiber:** 0 g

Approximate values for a 6 oz serving.

💧 Pitmaster Tip

When the burnt ends hit that glossy, tacky stage, pull them right away — too long and the sugar burns instead of caramelizes.

📓 Victory Notes

How did it turn out?

....

....

Next time I'll try it with:

....

....

"You don't need brisket to earn respect — just smoke and sugar."

CHICKEN CHAMPIONS

ITALIAN DRESSING CHICKEN BREASTS

When in doubt, pour and grill.

Prep: 10 min   Cook: 12 min   Serves: 4

YOU'LL NEED

- 4 boneless, skinless chicken breasts (about 2½–3 lb total)
- ½ cup Italian dressing (store-bought or homemade)

Two ingredients. Infinite flavor. No excuses.

HOW TO MAKE IT

1. **Place** chicken in a dish or resealable bag and **pour** dressing over to coat.
2. **Marinate** at least 15 minutes — or up to 3 hours if you've got time.
3. **Preheat** grill to medium-high (around 400 °F).
4. **Grill** 5–6 minutes per side, flipping once, until internal temp hits 165 °F.
5. **Rest** a few minutes before serving to lock in the juices.

⚙ GRILL FUEL STATS (per serving)

Calories: 255 | **Protein:** 33 g | **Fat:** 12 g | **Carbs:** 2 g | **Sugar:** 1 g | **Fiber:** 0 g
Approximate values for one 6 oz chicken breast.

Pitmaster Tip

The longer the marinade, the bolder the bite — Italian dressing tenderizes and flavors at the same time.

Victory Notes

How did it turn out?

....

....

Next time I'll try it with:

....

....

"Never underestimate bottled brilliance."

HONEY CHIPOTLE CHICKEN THIGHS

Sweet fire, sticky fingers, and zero regrets.

Prep: 15 min   Cook: 15 min   Serves: 4

YOU'LL NEED

- 6 boneless chicken thighs
- 3 tbsp honey
- 2 tbsp chipotle peppers in adobo, chopped
- 2 tsp minced garlic
- 3 tbsp vegetable oil

Five ingredients. All attitude.

HOW TO MAKE IT

1. **Whisk** oil, honey, chopped chipotles, and garlic with a pinch of salt.
2. **Add** chicken to a bowl or bag, toss to coat, and marinate at least 30 minutes (or overnight for more kick).
3. **Preheat** grill to medium-high.
4. **Grill** thighs 5–7 minutes per side, basting once with leftover marinade.
5. **Rest** 3 minutes before serving. Sticky heat = perfect finish.

☼ GRILL FUEL STATS (per serving)

Calories: 370 | **Protein:** 33 g | **Fat:** 19 g | **Carbs:** 14 g | **Sugar:** 12 g | **Fiber:** 0 g

Approximate values for 2 thighs per serving.

⬤ Pitmaster Tip

Save a spoonful of that marinade and drizzle it over grilled corn — it'll change your life.

▦ Victory Notes

How did it turn out?

....

....

Next time I'll try it with:

....

....

"If it burns a little, you're doing it right."

LEMON HERB GRILLED CHICKEN

Light, juicy, and proof that simple still wins.

Prep: 10 min   Cook: 12 min   Serves: 4

YOU'LL NEED

- 2 lb chicken breasts or thighs
- 3 tbsp olive oil
- 1 lemon, juiced
- 3 tsp minced garlic
- 3 tsp Italian seasoning (or mixed dried herbs)

Five ingredients. Classic flavor that never fails.

HOW TO MAKE IT

1. **Whisk** olive oil, lemon juice, garlic, and herbs with a pinch of salt and pepper.
2. **Coat** chicken evenly with marinade and let rest for at least 30 minutes (up to overnight).
3. **Preheat** grill to medium-high.
4. **Grill** chicken 5–6 minutes per side, or until internal temp hits 165 °F.
5. **Rest** 5 minutes before slicing — tender, citrusy perfection.

☼ GRILL FUEL STATS (per serving)

Calories: 280 | **Protein:** 36 g | **Fat:** 13 g | **Carbs:** 2 g | **Sugar:** 0 g | **Fiber:** 0 g

Approximate values for one 6 oz chicken portion.

◌ Pitmaster Tip

Add lemon slices directly to the grill beside the chicken — they caramelize and make a killer garnish.

▦ Victory Notes

How did it turn out?

....

....

Next time I'll try it with:

....

....

"Bright, bold, and built for the grill."

CHILI LIME CHICKEN DRUMSTICKS

Tangy heat that sticks to your fingers and your memory.

Prep: 10 min   Cook: 35 min   Serves: 4

YOU'LL NEED

- 8 chicken drumsticks
- 3 tbsp vegetable oil
- 1 lime, juiced
- 2 tsp chili powder
- ¼ cup chopped cilantro (for garnish)

Five ingredients. No napkin can save you.

HOW TO MAKE IT

1. **Mix** oil, lime juice, and chili powder in a large bowl with a pinch of salt.
2. **Add** drumsticks and toss to coat evenly. Marinate 20–30 minutes while the grill heats.
3. **Preheat** grill to medium heat (about 375 °F).
4. **Grill** drumsticks 30–35 minutes total, turning every 6–7 minutes, until golden and juices run clear.
5. **Finish** with a squeeze of lime and a scatter of cilantro.

☼ GRILL FUEL STATS (per serving)

Calories: 290 | **Protein:** 30 g | **Fat:** 17 g | **Carbs:** 2 g | **Sugar:** 0 g |
Fiber: 0 g
Approximate values for 2 drumsticks per serving.

○ Pitmaster Tip

For an extra kick, zest the lime before juicing it and add the zest to your
marinade — pure flavor bomb.

☷ Victory Notes

How did it turn out?

....

....

Next time I'll try it with:

....

....

"When life gives you limes, light the grill."

BROWN SUGAR GARLIC CHICKEN

Sweet. Savory. Sticky. And stupidly easy.

Prep: 10 min   Cook: 15 min   Serves: 4

YOU'LL NEED

- 2 lb chicken thighs or breasts
- ⅓ cup brown sugar (packed)
- ¼ cup soy sauce
- 3 tsp minced garlic
- ½ tsp black pepper

Five ingredients. Fifteen minutes. Flavor explosion.

HOW TO MAKE IT

1. **Whisk** brown sugar, soy sauce, garlic, and pepper in a bowl until the sugar dissolves.
2. **Add** chicken and toss to coat evenly. Marinate 30 minutes if you've got time.
3. **Preheat** grill to medium heat (around 375 °F).
4. **Grill** chicken 6 minutes per side, brushing once with leftover marinade.
5. **Rest** 5 minutes before serving. The glaze will thicken into perfection.

GRILL FUEL STATS (per serving)

Calories: 340 | **Protein:** 32 g | **Fat:** 15 g | **Carbs:** 18 g | **Sugar:** 15 g | **Fiber:** 0 g

Approximate values for a 6 oz serving.

Pitmaster Tip

Reserve a few tablespoons of the marinade before adding chicken — simmer it for 2 minutes and drizzle over the finished dish for extra shine.

Victory Notes

How did it turn out?

....

....

Next time I'll try it with:

....

....

"If it's not sticky, you didn't cook it long enough."

GREEK YOGURT LEMON CHICKEN

Tangy, juicy, and tender enough to impress anyone.

Prep: 10 min   Cook: 12 min   Serves: 4

YOU'LL NEED

- 2 lb chicken breasts or thighs
- ⅓ cup plain Greek yogurt
- 2 cloves garlic, minced
- 1 lemon (zest and juice)
- 1 tsp salt

Five ingredients. Marinated magic.

HOW TO MAKE IT

1. **Mix** Greek yogurt, garlic, lemon zest, lemon juice, and salt in a bowl.
2. **Add** chicken and coat well with the mixture. Marinate at least 30 minutes (up to 8 hours).
3. **Preheat** grill to medium-high (about 400 °F).
4. **Wipe off** excess marinade (to avoid flare-ups) and grill 5–6 minutes per side.
5. **Rest** 5 minutes before slicing — juicy, citrusy perfection.

GRILL FUEL STATS (per serving)

Calories: 300 | **Protein:** 37 g | **Fat:** 13 g | **Carbs:** 3 g | **Sugar:** 1 g | **Fiber:** 0 g
Approximate values for one 6 oz chicken portion.

Pitmaster Tip

Use full-fat yogurt — it tenderizes better and helps build a light charred crust on the grill.

Victory Notes

How did it turn out?

....

....

Next time I'll try it with:

....

....

"Yogurt: the secret weapon your grill never saw coming."

BEER CAN CHICKEN

The one that turns heads and makes legends.

Prep: 15 min   Cook: 1 hr 15 min   Serves: 4–6

YOU'LL NEED

- 1 whole chicken (4–5 lb)
- 2 tbsp olive oil
- 1 tbsp kosher salt
- 2 tsp black pepper
- 1 tsp dried thyme
- 1 can beer (12 oz, half-full — for the throne)

Five ingredients, one mighty bird, and a can of courage.

HOW TO MAKE IT

1. **Preheat** grill to medium (around 350 °F) for indirect cooking.
2. **Rub** the chicken all over (and inside the cavity) with olive oil, salt, pepper, and thyme.
3. **Drink or pour out** half the beer, then slide the open can into the cavity — the chicken should sit upright.
4. **Grill** over indirect heat for 1¼–1½ hours, until internal temp hits 165 °F in the breast.
5. **Rest** 10 minutes before carefully lifting the bird off the can (use tongs and a towel — it's hot). Slice and serve proudly.

⚙ **GRILL FUEL STATS (per serving)**

Calories: 410 | **Protein:** 48 g | **Fat:** 22 g | **Carbs:** 0 g | **Sugar:** 0 g | **Fiber:** 0 g

Approximate values for one 6 oz serving with skin.

◌ Pitmaster Tip

Swap beer for ginger ale or cola for a sweeter steam and a caramelized glaze on the skin.

▤ Victory Notes

How did it turn out?

....

....

Next time I'll try it with:

....

....

"Give a man a beer, and he'll drink. Give his chicken a beer, and he'll brag forever."

GRILLED BUFFALO WINGS

Fire, smoke, and a little chaos — the right way to eat chicken.

Prep: 15 min   Cook: 25 min   Serves: 4

YOU'LL NEED

- 2 lb chicken wings (split, tips removed)
- ¼ cup hot sauce (Frank's RedHot or similar)
- 3 tbsp melted butter
- 1 tbsp vinegar (white or apple cider)
- ½ tsp garlic powder

Five ingredients. No fryer. No mercy.

HOW TO MAKE IT

1. **Preheat** grill to medium-high (about 400 °F).
2. **Season** wings lightly with salt and pepper, then **grill** 20–25 minutes, turning often, until crispy and cooked through.
3. **Melt** butter in a bowl, then whisk in hot sauce, vinegar, and garlic powder.
4. **Toss** grilled wings in the sauce until coated and glossy.
5. **Serve** immediately with a cold drink and zero shame.

☼ GRILL FUEL STATS (per serving)

Calories: 360 | **Protein:** 31 g | **Fat:** 25 g | **Carbs:** 2 g | **Sugar:** 1 g | **Fiber:** 0 g

Approximate values for ½ lb wings per serving.

◌ Pitmaster Tip

Grill wings on indirect heat first, then finish directly over the flames for that final crackling skin.

▤ Victory Notes

How did it turn out?

....

....

Next time I'll try it with:

....

....

"If your lips aren't tingling, turn up the heat."

BACON-WRAPPED CHICKEN BREASTS

Because everything's better when it's wearing bacon.

Prep: 15 min   Cook: 25 min   Serves: 4

YOU'LL NEED

- 4 boneless, skinless chicken breasts
- 8 slices bacon
- 3 tbsp brown sugar
- 2 tbsp soy sauce
- 1 tsp smoked paprika

Five ingredients. One reason to grill all weekend.

HOW TO MAKE IT

1. **Preheat** grill to medium heat (around 375 °F).
2. **Mix** brown sugar, soy sauce, and smoked paprika into a quick glaze.
3. **Wrap** each chicken breast with two bacon slices, securing ends underneath.
4. **Brush** with glaze and grill 10–12 minutes per side, turning gently until bacon is crisp and chicken hits 165 °F inside.
5. **Rest** 5 minutes before slicing — sticky, smoky perfection.

☼ GRILL FUEL STATS (per serving)

Calories: 420 | **Protein:** 38 g | **Fat:** 24 g | **Carbs:** 8 g | **Sugar:** 7 g | **Fiber:** 0 g

Approximate values for one bacon-wrapped chicken breast.

◌ Pitmaster Tip

Start on indirect heat so the bacon renders without burning — then finish over direct flame for that crispy char.

▦ Victory Notes

How did it turn out?

....

....

Next time I'll try it with:

....

....

"Bacon: the official uniform of heroes."

SMOKED BBQ CHICKEN THIGHS

Low smoke. High reward. Every bite a trophy.

Prep: 15 min   Cook: 1 hr 15 min   Serves: 4–6

YOU'LL NEED

- 6 bone-in, skin-on chicken thighs
- 3 tbsp olive oil
- 2 tbsp BBQ seasoning or rub
- ½ cup barbecue sauce
- 1 tbsp honey

Five ingredients. All glory.

HOW TO MAKE IT

1. **Preheat** smoker to 250 °F using apple or hickory wood.
2. **Rub** thighs with olive oil and BBQ seasoning until evenly coated.
3. **Smoke** skin-side up for about 1 hour, or until internal temp hits 160 °F.
4. **Brush** with BBQ sauce mixed with honey, then **increase** heat to 350 °F for 10–15 minutes to caramelize the glaze.
5. **Rest** 5 minutes before serving. Sticky. Smoky. Irresistible.

☼ GRILL FUEL STATS (per serving)

Calories: 380 | **Protein:** 34 g | **Fat:** 20 g | **Carbs:** 14 g | **Sugar:** 11 g | **Fiber:** 0 g

Approximate values for one large thigh with glaze.

⬤ Pitmaster Tip

Crispier skin? Smoke uncovered the whole time — moisture is the enemy of crunch.

☰ Victory Notes

How did it turn out?

....

....

Next time I'll try it with:

....

....

"Smoke first. Sauce later. Always."

PORK LEGENDS

EASY BBQ PORK RIBS

Low effort. High praise. Sticky fingers guaranteed.

Prep: 15 min   Cook: 2 hr   Serves: 4–6

YOU'LL NEED

- 2 racks baby back or St. Louis–style pork ribs
- ½ cup BBQ rub or seasoning blend
- 1 cup barbecue sauce
- 2 tbsp apple cider vinegar
- 2 tbsp honey

Five ingredients. The kind of ribs that make neighbors jealous.

HOW TO MAKE IT

1. **Preheat** grill or smoker to 275 °F for indirect cooking.

2. **Remove** membrane from rib backs, then rub both sides generously with BBQ seasoning.

3. **Smoke** or grill for 1½ hours, brushing with a mix of barbecue sauce, vinegar, and honey during the last 30 minutes.

4. **Check** for tenderness — the ribs should bend easily but not fall apart.

5. **Rest** 10 minutes before slicing. Serve sauced and proud.

☼ GRILL FUEL STATS (per serving)

Calories: 520 | **Protein:** 35 g | **Fat:** 32 g | **Carbs:** 18 g | **Sugar:** 15 g | **Fiber:** 0 g

Approximate values for ½ rack per serving.

◐ Pitmaster Tip

Wrap ribs in foil with a tablespoon of apple cider vinegar midway for ultra-tender results — it's your secret cheat to "fall-off-the-bone."

▤ Victory Notes

How did it turn out?

....

....

Next time I'll try it with:

....

....

"Sticky hands. Silent guests. That's victory."

SMOKED PULLED PORK SHOULDER

Low and slow turns ordinary pork into a legend.

Prep: 20 min   Cook: 8–10 hr   Serves: 10–12

YOU'LL NEED

- 1 pork shoulder or Boston butt (6–8 lb)
- 3 tbsp yellow mustard
- ½ cup BBQ dry rub
- 1 cup apple juice (for spritzing)
- ½ cup barbecue sauce

Five ingredients. One mission: melt-in-your-mouth perfection.

HOW TO MAKE IT

1. **Preheat** smoker to 250 °F using hickory or apple wood.
2. **Rub** pork with mustard, then coat evenly with BBQ rub.
3. **Smoke** for 6–8 hours, spritzing with apple juice every 60–90 minutes.
4. **Wrap** in foil once internal temp hits 165 °F, then continue to 200–205 °F.
5. **Rest** 1 hour before shredding. Mix pulled meat with barbecue sauce right before serving.

⚙ GRILL FUEL STATS (per serving)

Calories: 420 | **Protein:** 39 g | **Fat:** 27 g | **Carbs:** 6 g | **Sugar:** 5 g | **Fiber:** 0 g

Approximate values for a 6 oz serving with sauce.

◐ Pitmaster Tip

For maximum bark, unwrap during the final 30 minutes to let the surface firm up and caramelize.

▤ Victory Notes

How did it turn out?

....

....

Next time I'll try it with:

....

....

"Time, smoke, and patience — the holy trinity of pork."

SOY & BROWN SUGAR PORK CHOPS

Sweet, smoky, and ready before your second beer.

Prep: 10 min   Cook: 15 min   Serves: 4

YOU'LL NEED

- 4 pork chops (bone-in or boneless, about 1 inch thick)
- ¼ cup soy sauce
- ¼ cup brown sugar
- 2 tsp minced garlic
- 1 tbsp olive oil

Five ingredients. One bite and you're hooked.

HOW TO MAKE IT

1. **Whisk** soy sauce, brown sugar, garlic, and olive oil until the sugar dissolves.
2. **Pour** over pork chops in a dish or bag, coating evenly. Marinate 30 minutes to 2 hours.
3. **Preheat** grill to medium-high heat (around 400 °F).
4. **Grill** chops 5–6 minutes per side, brushing once with leftover marinade.
5. **Rest** 5 minutes before serving — caramelized edges guaranteed.

⚙ GRILL FUEL STATS (per serving)

Calories: 340 | **Protein:** 33 g | **Fat:** 17 g | **Carbs:** 10 g | **Sugar:** 8 g | **Fiber:** 0 g
Approximate values for one 6 oz chop.

◐ Pitmaster Tip

Sprinkle a pinch of crushed red pepper into the marinade for a subtle kick that balances the sweetness.

▤ Victory Notes

How did it turn out?

....

....

Next time I'll try it with:

....

....

"Fast food wishes it smelled like this."

BACON-WRAPPED PORK TENDERLOIN (MUSTARD GLAZE)

Classy enough for guests. Easy enough for Tuesday.

Prep: 15 min   Cook: 30–35 min   Serves: 4–6

YOU'LL NEED

- 1 pork tenderloin (about 1½ lb)
- 6–8 slices bacon
- 3 tbsp Dijon mustard
- 2 tbsp brown sugar
- 1 tbsp apple cider vinegar

Five ingredients. One flawless roast.

HOW TO MAKE IT

1. **Preheat** grill to 375 °F (medium heat).
2. **Mix** Dijon mustard, brown sugar, and vinegar into a quick glaze.
3. **Wrap** the tenderloin with bacon slices, tucking ends underneath.
4. **Brush** the whole thing with the mustard glaze.
5. **Grill** over indirect heat for 25–30 minutes, turning occasionally, until internal temp reaches 145 °F.

6. **Rest** 10 minutes before slicing into juicy perfection.

⚙ GRILL FUEL STATS (per serving)

Calories: 390 | **Protein:** 37 g | **Fat:** 23 g | **Carbs:** 6 g | **Sugar:** 5 g | **Fiber:** 0 g

Approximate values for a 6 oz serving.

◔ Pitmaster Tip

Brush the glaze twice — once before grilling, and again during the final 5 minutes for that sticky, caramelized finish.

▤ Victory Notes

How did it turn out?

....

....

Next time I'll try it with:

....

....

"If bacon's the suit, mustard's the tie."

PORK BELLY BURNT ENDS

Smoked candy for carnivores.

Prep: 20 min   Cook: 3 hr   Serves: 6–8

YOU'LL NEED

- 3 lb pork belly, skin removed and cut into 1½-inch cubes
- ¼ cup BBQ rub
- ½ cup barbecue sauce
- ¼ cup honey
- ¼ cup brown sugar

Five ingredients. Infinite flavor.

HOW TO MAKE IT

1. **Preheat** smoker to 250 °F using fruit wood (apple or cherry).
2. **Toss** pork belly cubes in BBQ rub until fully coated.
3. **Smoke** for 2 hours on a wire rack, uncovered, until the fat starts to render and edges darken.
4. **Transfer** cubes to a foil pan and mix with barbecue sauce, honey, and brown sugar.
5. **Cover** and smoke 1 more hour, then **uncover** for the last 20 minutes to caramelize.

⚙ GRILL FUEL STATS (per serving)

Calories: 590 | **Protein:** 29 g | **Fat:** 48 g | **Carbs:** 12 g | **Sugar:** 10 g |
Fiber: 0 g
Approximate values for a 6 oz serving.

⬤ Pitmaster Tip

For a restaurant-quality glaze, reduce leftover sauce from the pan over
medium heat until thick and sticky — then drizzle it over the finished cubes.

▤ Victory Notes

How did it turn out?

....

....

Next time I'll try it with:

....

....

*"This is what happens when smoke meets sugar and refuses to
quit."*

GREEK PORK SOUVLAKI SKEWERS

Juicy, herby, and kissed by the flame.

Prep: 15 min   Cook: 10–12 min   Serves: 4

YOU'LL NEED

- 1½ lb pork shoulder or loin, cut into 1½-inch cubes
- 3 tbsp olive oil
- 1 lemon, juiced
- 2 tsp dried oregano
- 3 cloves garlic, minced

Five ingredients. One trip to the Greek isles — no passport required.

HOW TO MAKE IT

1. **Whisk** olive oil, lemon juice, oregano, and garlic in a bowl with a pinch of salt and pepper.
2. **Add** pork cubes, toss to coat, and marinate 30 minutes (or overnight for richer flavor).
3. **Thread** pork onto skewers.
4. **Grill** over medium-high heat for 10–12 minutes, turning occasionally until golden and cooked through.
5. **Rest** 5 minutes, then squeeze a little extra lemon over the top before serving.

GRILL FUEL STATS (per serving)

Calories: 320 | **Protein:** 33 g | **Fat:** 19 g | **Carbs:** 2 g | **Sugar:** 0 g | **Fiber:** 0 g

Approximate values for ¼ of total yield.

Pitmaster Tip

Serve it with warm pita and a side of plain Greek yogurt mixed with a squeeze of lemon — it doubles as the world's easiest tzatziki.

Victory Notes

How did it turn out?

....

....

Next time I'll try it with:

....

....

"Smoke, lemon, and oregano — the real Mediterranean trinity."

HOT DOG BURNT ENDS

The poor man's brisket cubes — and proud of it.

Prep: 5 min   Cook: 1 hr   Serves: 6

YOU'LL NEED

- 2 packs hot dogs (about 16 total)
- ¼ cup BBQ rub
- ½ cup barbecue sauce
- 3 tbsp brown sugar
- 2 tbsp honey

Five ingredients. Maximum chaos. Endless smiles.

HOW TO MAKE IT

1. **Preheat** smoker or grill to 250 °F using fruit wood (apple or cherry works great).

2. **Cut** hot dogs into 1½-inch chunks and toss in BBQ rub until coated.

3. **Smoke** for 30 minutes on a foil tray to let the edges crisp slightly.

4. **Mix** barbecue sauce, brown sugar, and honey, then **toss** with the smoked hot dog pieces.

5. **Return** to the grill for another 20–30 minutes, uncovered, until sticky, glazed, and irresistible.

⚙ GRILL FUEL STATS (per serving)

Calories: 310 | **Protein:** 10 g | **Fat:** 22 g | **Carbs:** 14 g | **Sugar:** 12 g | **Fiber:** 0 g

Approximate values for about 5–6 pieces.

◔ Pitmaster Tip

Use high-quality all-beef hot dogs — they crisp better, taste smokier, and hold that sweet glaze without turning mushy.

▮ Victory Notes

How did it turn out?

....

....

Next time I'll try it with:

....

....

"Don't knock it till you've smoked it."

BEER-BRAISED BRATWURST

Foamy, flavorful, and perfectly charred — a beer in both hands kind of meal.

Prep: 10 min   Cook: 25 min   Serves: 4–6

YOU'LL NEED

- 6 bratwurst sausages
- 1 large onion, sliced
- 2 cups beer (lager or pale ale works best)
- 2 tbsp butter
- 1 tbsp Dijon mustard

Five ingredients. Half the effort. All the applause.

HOW TO MAKE IT

1. **Melt** butter in a cast-iron pan over medium heat on your grill.
2. **Add** onions and sauté until soft and golden.
3. **Pour** in beer and stir in Dijon mustard. Bring to a simmer.
4. **Add** bratwursts and **simmer** 10–12 minutes until cooked through.
5. **Transfer** brats directly to the grill grates and **char** 2–3 minutes per side for that smoky snap.

⚙ GRILL FUEL STATS (per serving)

Calories: 420 | **Protein:** 20 g | **Fat:** 33 g | **Carbs:** 8 g | **Sugar:** 2 g |
Fiber: 0 g
Approximate values for one brat with onions.

🔥 Pitmaster Tip

Toss the leftover beer-onion mix back over the grilled brats before serving —
it turns into a malty, buttery glaze that's absurdly good.

📜 Victory Notes

How did it turn out?

....

....

Next time I'll try it with:

....

....

"If it sizzles in beer, it belongs on the grill."

SMOKED BONE-IN PORK CHOPS

Big bones, bigger flavor — pure backyard glory.

Prep: 10 min   Cook: 1 hr   Serves: 4

YOU'LL NEED

- 4 thick-cut bone-in pork chops (about 1 inch thick)
- 3 tbsp olive oil
- 3 tbsp BBQ rub or seasoning
- ½ cup apple juice (for spritzing or moisture pan)
- ¼ cup barbecue sauce

Five ingredients. One smoky masterpiece.

HOW TO MAKE IT

1. **Preheat** smoker to 250 °F using apple or hickory wood.
2. **Rub** chops with olive oil, then coat both sides generously with BBQ rub.
3. **Smoke** for 45–60 minutes, spritzing once or twice with apple juice to stay moist.
4. **Brush** with barbecue sauce and raise temperature to 350 °F for the last 10 minutes to glaze.
5. **Rest** 5 minutes before serving. Juicy inside, bark on the outside — perfection.

⚙ GRILL FUEL STATS (per serving)

Calories: 410 | **Protein:** 41 g | **Fat:** 24 g | **Carbs:** 8 g | **Sugar:** 6 g | **Fiber:** 0 g

Approximate values for one 8 oz chop with glaze.

◐ Pitmaster Tip

To nail that "smoke ring," keep the chops cold when they hit the grill — condensation helps smoke stick to the surface early on.

▣ Victory Notes

How did it turn out?

....

....

Next time I'll try it with:

....

....

"Thick chops, slow smoke, zero regrets."

FISH & FLAME

SOY & BROWN SUGAR GRILLED SALMON

Sticky glaze. Smoky char. Five ingredients of genius.

Prep: 10 min   Cook: 12 min   Serves: 4

YOU'LL NEED

- 4 salmon fillets (about 6 oz each)
- ¼ cup soy sauce
- ¼ cup brown sugar (packed)
- 2 tbsp olive oil
- 1 clove garlic, minced

Five ingredients. Restaurant results — backyard effort.

HOW TO MAKE IT

1. **Whisk** soy sauce, brown sugar, olive oil, and garlic until smooth.
2. **Marinate** salmon fillets skin-side down for 20–30 minutes (keep cool).
3. **Preheat** grill to medium-high (about 400 °F).
4. **Grill** salmon 5–6 minutes skin-side down, then flip gently and cook 2–3 more minutes until just opaque.
5. **Brush** with remaining marinade during the last minute for a glossy glaze.

⚙ GRILL FUEL STATS (per serving)

Calories: 360 | **Protein:** 34 g | **Fat:** 20 g | **Carbs:** 10 g | **Sugar:** 8 g | **Fiber:** 0 g

Approximate values for one 6 oz fillet with glaze.

◔ Pitmaster Tip

For perfect char, oil the grates just before you lay down the fish — and never touch it until it releases easily.

▤ Victory Notes

How did it turn out?

....

....

Next time I'll try it with:

....

....

"The ocean's answer to BBQ ribs."

GARLIC BUTTER SHRIMP SKEWERS

Five ingredients. Ten minutes. Infinite approval.

Prep: 10 min   Cook: 6–8 min   Serves: 4

YOU'LL NEED

- 1 lb large shrimp, peeled and deveined
- ¼ cup butter, melted
- 3 cloves garlic, minced
- 1 tbsp lemon juice
- 1 tbsp chopped parsley (fresh or dried)

Five ingredients. Straight-up flavor bomb.

HOW TO MAKE IT

1. **Preheat** grill to medium-high (about 400 °F).
2. **Mix** melted butter, garlic, lemon juice, and parsley in a bowl.
3. **Thread** shrimp onto skewers and brush generously with the butter mixture.
4. **Grill** 2–3 minutes per side until pink and slightly charred.
5. **Brush** again with leftover butter right before serving.

 **GRILL FUEL STATS (per serving)**

Calories: 230 | **Protein:** 25 g | **Fat:** 13 g | **Carbs:** 2 g | **Sugar:** 0 g | **Fiber:** 0 g

Approximate values for ¼ lb shrimp per serving.

◌ Pitmaster Tip

Use metal skewers or double up bamboo ones — shrimp flip better and stay juicy when they don't spin.

▥ Victory Notes

How did it turn out?

....

....

Next time I'll try it with:

....

....

"Butter, garlic, and flame — the holy trinity of seafood."

LEMONY HERB GRILLED HALIBUT

Clean, bright, and proof that "healthy" can taste heroic.

Prep: 10 min   Cook: 10 min   Serves: 4

YOU'LL NEED

- 4 halibut fillets (about 6 oz each)
- 3 tbsp olive oil
- 2 tbsp lemon juice
- 2 tsp minced garlic
- 2 tsp dried herbs (thyme, parsley, or Italian mix)

Five ingredients. All class. Zero compromise.

HOW TO MAKE IT

1. **Preheat** grill to medium-high (400 °F).
2. **Whisk** olive oil, lemon juice, garlic, and herbs in a small bowl with a pinch of salt and pepper.
3. **Brush** halibut fillets on both sides with the mixture.
4. **Grill** 4–5 minutes per side until flaky and just opaque.
5. **Drizzle** remaining marinade over the top before serving.

⚙ **GRILL FUEL STATS (per serving)**

Calories: 290 | **Protein:** 38 g | **Fat:** 14 g | **Carbs:** 1 g | **Sugar:** 0 g | **Fiber:** 0 g
Approximate values for one 6 oz fillet.

Pitmaster Tip

Lay the fish on a thin lemon slice "bed" to prevent sticking and add extra aroma — it's the pro move no one tells you.

Victory Notes

How did it turn out?

....

....

Next time I'll try it with:

....

....

"Citrus and flame — nature's way of saying you nailed it."

BACON-WRAPPED SCALLOPS

Land meets sea — and everything tastes better for it.

Prep: 15 min   Cook: 10–12 min   Serves: 4

YOU'LL NEED

- 12 large sea scallops
- 6 slices bacon, cut in half
- 2 tbsp olive oil
- 1 tbsp lemon juice
- 1 tsp black pepper

Five ingredients. Fancy results. Grill simplicity.

HOW TO MAKE IT

1. **Preheat** grill to medium-high (about 400 °F).
2. **Wrap** each scallop with half a bacon slice and secure with a toothpick.
3. **Whisk** olive oil, lemon juice, and pepper; brush over the scallops.
4. **Grill** 4–5 minutes per side, turning gently, until bacon is crisp and scallops are opaque in the center.
5. **Rest** 2 minutes before serving — they'll finish cooking in their own heat.

☼ GRILL FUEL STATS (per serving)

Calories: 310 | **Protein:** 24 g | **Fat:** 22 g | **Carbs:** 2 g | **Sugar:** 0 g | **Fiber:** 0 g

Approximate values for 3 scallops per serving.

◊ Pitmaster Tip

Precook bacon halfway before wrapping — it'll crisp up perfectly without overcooking the scallops.

▤ Victory Notes

How did it turn out?

....

....

Next time I'll try it with:

....

....

"When bacon hugs seafood, the world makes sense."

GRILLED LOBSTER TAILS WITH GARLIC BUTTER

Luxury meets flame — five ingredients to impress anyone.

Prep: 15 min   Cook: 10 min   Serves: 4

YOU'LL NEED

- 4 lobster tails (about 6 oz each)
- ¼ cup butter, melted
- 2 cloves garlic, minced
- 1 tbsp lemon juice
- 1 tsp paprika

Five ingredients. Restaurant flavor, backyard effort.

HOW TO MAKE IT

1. **Preheat** grill to medium-high (400 °F).
2. **Split** lobster tails lengthwise with kitchen shears; gently lift meat over the shell for easy grilling.
3. **Whisk** butter, garlic, lemon juice, and paprika.

4. **Brush** the lobster meat generously and **grill** shell-side down 5–6 minutes, then flip and cook 2–3 minutes more, basting with extra butter until opaque and lightly charred.

5. **Serve** immediately with any leftover garlic butter drizzled on top.

○ GRILL FUEL STATS (per serving)

Calories: 340 | **Protein:** 35 g | **Fat:** 21 g | **Carbs:** 1 g | **Sugar:** 0 g | **Fiber:** 0 g
Approximate values for one 6 oz tail with butter glaze.

○ Pitmaster Tip

For extra presentation points, finish with a quick squeeze of lemon and a pinch of sea salt right off the grill — it makes the butter pop.

▤ Victory Notes

How did it turn out?

....

....

Next time I'll try it with:

....

....

"Flame and butter — the language of kings."

SOY-GINGER GRILLED TUNA STEAKS

Simple. Bold. Five ingredients, endless flavor.

Prep: 10 min   Cook: 8 min   Serves: 4

YOU'LL NEED

- 4 tuna steaks (about 6 oz each)
- ¼ cup soy sauce
- 2 tbsp olive oil
- 1 tbsp grated fresh ginger (or 1 tsp ground)
- 1 tbsp honey

Five ingredients. Straight power food.

HOW TO MAKE IT

1. **Whisk** soy sauce, olive oil, ginger, and honey until smooth.
2. **Marinate** tuna steaks for 15–20 minutes — no longer, or the soy will "cook" the edges.
3. **Preheat** grill to high heat (around 450–500 °F).
4. **Grill** 2–3 minutes per side for medium-rare, or longer if preferred.
5. **Brush** once more with the marinade right before serving for a glossy finish.

☼ GRILL FUEL STATS (per serving)

Calories: 310 | **Protein:** 42 g | **Fat:** 13 g | **Carbs:** 4 g | **Sugar:** 3 g | **Fiber:** 0 g

Approximate values for one 6 oz tuna steak.

◔ Pitmaster Tip

Sear tuna fast and hot — if it flakes like salmon, you went too long. Pink in the center means perfection.

▤ Victory Notes

How did it turn out?

....

....

Next time I'll try it with:

....

....

"Fire. Soy. Ginger. Respect."

CITRUS GARLIC SWORDFISH

The steak lover's seafood — grilled to golden perfection.

Prep: 10 min   Cook: 10–12 min   Serves: 4

YOU'LL NEED

- 4 swordfish steaks (about 6 oz each)
- 3 tbsp olive oil
- 1 orange, juiced (or mix of orange & lemon)
- 2 cloves garlic, minced
- 1 tsp dried thyme or rosemary

Five ingredients. Pure sunshine on a grill.

HOW TO MAKE IT

1. **Whisk** olive oil, citrus juice, garlic, and thyme with a pinch of salt and pepper.
2. **Brush** both sides of swordfish generously with the mixture.
3. **Preheat** grill to medium-high (400 °F).
4. **Grill** 4–5 minutes per side until just opaque and grill-marked.
5. **Drizzle** any remaining marinade over hot steaks right before serving.

GRILL FUEL STATS (per serving)

Calories: 340 | **Protein:** 42 g | **Fat:** 18 g | **Carbs:** 3 g | **Sugar:** 2 g | **Fiber:** 0 g

Approximate values for one 6 oz swordfish steak.

Pitmaster Tip

Swordfish dries fast — pull it at 140 °F internal and let it rest. The carry-over heat will finish it perfectly juicy.

Victory Notes

How did it turn out?

....

....

Next time I'll try it with:

....

....

"Citrus, garlic, and flame — simple. Strong. Sublime."

GARLIC-BUTTER GRILLED CLAMS

Smoky, buttery, and made for sharing straight off the grill.

Prep: 10 min   Cook: 8–10 min   Serves: 4

YOU'LL NEED

- 2 lb fresh clams (littlenecks or manila)
- ¼ cup butter, melted
- 3 cloves garlic, minced
- 1 tbsp lemon juice
- 1 tbsp chopped parsley (fresh or dried)

Five ingredients. One unforgettable aroma.

HOW TO MAKE IT

1. **Preheat** grill to medium-high (around 400 °F).
2. **Rinse** clams under cold water and discard any that stay open when tapped.
3. **Whisk** butter, garlic, lemon juice, and parsley in a small bowl.
4. **Place** clams directly on the grill grate (hinge side down).
5. **Grill** 5–7 minutes until they open — then **spoon** the garlic butter into each shell and grill 1–2 minutes more until sizzling.
6. **Serve** immediately with a squeeze of lemon or crusty bread if desired.

GRILL FUEL STATS (per serving)

Calories: 260 | **Protein:** 22 g | **Fat:** 16 g | **Carbs:** 4 g | **Sugar:** 1 g | **Fiber:** 0 g

Approximate values for ½ lb of clams per person.

Pitmaster Tip

Keep the lid closed while the clams cook — it traps the smoky heat that infuses them with flavor before they open.

Victory Notes

How did it turn out?

....

....

Next time I'll try it with:

....

....

"When the shells pop, happiness is served."

WHOLE GRILLED TROUT (LEMON & THYME)

Simple. Fragrant. Proof that perfection needs only five ingredients.

Prep: 10 min   Cook: 12–15 min   Serves: 2–3

YOU'LL NEED

- 2 whole trout (cleaned, about 1 lb each)
- 2 tbsp olive oil
- 1 lemon, thinly sliced
- 4 sprigs fresh thyme (or 1 tsp dried)
- Salt & black pepper, to taste

Five ingredients. All natural. All flavor.

HOW TO MAKE IT

1. **Preheat** grill to medium-high (about 400 °F).
2. **Rinse and pat dry** trout, then rub inside and out with olive oil, salt, and pepper.
3. **Stuff** cavity with lemon slices and thyme sprigs.
4. **Grill** 5–7 minutes per side (use a fish basket or well-oiled grate) until skin crisps and flesh flakes easily.
5. **Drizzle** with a bit more olive oil and a squeeze of lemon before serving.

☼ GRILL FUEL STATS (per serving)

Calories: 330 | **Protein:** 37 g | **Fat:** 20 g | **Carbs:** 2 g | **Sugar:** 0 g | **Fiber:** 0 g
Approximate values for half a trout per serving.

◌ Pitmaster Tip

Use lemon slices under the trout to keep the skin from sticking — plus, they infuse the fish with delicate citrus steam.

▤ Victory Notes

How did it turn out?

....

....

Next time I'll try it with:

....

....

"From river to flame — fresh, fast, and full of soul."

SAUCES & RUBS

CLASSIC BBQ SAUCE (SWEET & TANGY)

The backbone of barbecue — five ingredients, endless glory.

Prep: 5 min   Cook: 15 min   Yields: About 2 cups

YOU'LL NEED

- 1 cup ketchup
- ¼ cup apple cider vinegar
- ¼ cup brown sugar
- 2 tbsp Worcestershire sauce
- 1 tsp smoked paprika

Five ingredients. All attitude.

HOW TO MAKE IT

1. **Combine** all ingredients in a saucepan over medium heat.
2. **Stir** until smooth and bring to a gentle simmer.
3. **Cook** 10–15 minutes, stirring often, until thickened slightly.
4. **Cool** before using — it'll thicken more as it rests.
5. **Store** in a jar in the fridge for up to 2 weeks.

SAUCE SPECS (per 2 tbsp)

Calories: 50 | **Protein:** 0 g | **Fat:** 0 g | **Carbs:** 13 g | **Sugar:** 11 g | **Fiber:** 0 g
Approximate values per serving.

◔ Pitmaster Tip

Add a teaspoon of hot sauce or liquid smoke to make it your own — it's the foundation, not the finish line.

▤ Victory Notes

How did it turn out?

....

....

Next time I'll tweak it with:

....

....

"Every pitmaster needs one sauce that never fails."

CAROLINA VINEGAR SAUCE

Tangy. Fiery. The soul of real Southern BBQ.

Prep: 5 min   Cook: 10 min   Yields: About 2 cups

YOU'LL NEED

- 1½ cups apple cider vinegar
- ½ cup ketchup
- 2 tbsp brown sugar
- 1 tbsp hot sauce (like Texas Pete or Tabasco)
- 1 tsp red pepper flakes

Five ingredients. Sharp enough to wake the neighbors.

HOW TO MAKE IT

1. **Combine** all ingredients in a saucepan over medium heat.
2. **Simmer** 8–10 minutes, stirring occasionally, until sugar dissolves and sauce slightly reduces.
3. **Cool** and store in a jar — flavors deepen after 24 hours.
4. **Shake** before using. Best brushed on pulled pork or drizzled over smoked ribs.

☼ SAUCE SPECS (per 2 tbsp)

Calories: 25 | **Protein:** 0 g | **Fat:** 0 g | **Carbs:** 6 g | **Sugar:** 5 g | **Fiber:** 0 g

Approximate values per serving.

◉ Pitmaster Tip

If you like it *real Carolina-style*, skip the ketchup completely for a clear vinegar sauce — then add a pinch more brown sugar for balance.

▣ Victory Notes

How did it turn out?

....

....

Next time I'll tweak it with:

....

....

"The bite that makes barbecue sing."

ALABAMA WHITE BBQ SAUCE

The smoky South's best-kept secret — creamy meets fire.

Prep: 5 min   Cook: 0 min   Yields: About 2 cups

YOU'LL NEED

- 1 cup mayonnaise
- ¼ cup apple cider vinegar
- 1 tbsp prepared horseradish
- 1 tbsp lemon juice
- 1 tsp black pepper

Five ingredients. No cooking. Pure Southern genius.

HOW TO MAKE IT

1. **Whisk** all ingredients in a bowl until smooth.
2. **Adjust** with extra vinegar or lemon juice for more tang.
3. **Chill** for at least 30 minutes to let flavors blend.
4. **Serve** brushed over smoked chicken or as a dipping sauce for ribs.
5. **Store** covered in the fridge up to 1 week.

☼ SAUCE SPECS (per 2 tbsp)

Calories: 120 | **Protein:** 0 g | **Fat:** 12 g | **Carbs:** 1 g | **Sugar:** 0 g | **Fiber:** 0 g
Approximate values per serving.

🔥 Pitmaster Tip

Add a dash of cayenne or smoked paprika for a pinkish tint and gentle heat — your secret twist on the classic.

📋 Victory Notes

How did it turn out? _____

Next time I'll tweak it with: _____

"Not all BBQ sauce is red — Alabama proved that."

ALL-PURPOSE BBQ DRY RUB

Your signature dust — five ingredients, endless glory.

Prep: 5 min   Cook: 0 min   Yields: About 1 cup

YOU'LL NEED

- ½ cup brown sugar
- 2 tbsp paprika (smoked or sweet)
- 1 tbsp salt
- 1 tbsp black pepper
- 1 tbsp garlic powder

Five ingredients. Instant pitmaster status.

HOW TO MAKE IT

1. **Mix** all ingredients in a bowl until evenly combined.
2. **Store** in an airtight jar for up to 6 months.
3. **Use** 1–2 tbsp per pound of meat before grilling or smoking.
4. **Massage** into meat 15–30 minutes before cooking for best flavor.

☼ **RUB SPECS (per tbsp)**

Calories: 35 | **Protein:** 0 g | **Fat:** 0 g | **Carbs:** 9 g | **Sugar:** 8 g | **Fiber:** 0 g

Approximate values per tablespoon.

◗ Pitmaster Tip

Add 1 tsp cayenne for heat or 1 tsp mustard powder for tang — tweak it until it's *yours*.

▤ Victory Notes

How did it turn out?

....

....

Next time I'll tweak it with:

....

....

"Before the sauce, there's the rub."

COFFEE STEAK RUB

Dark, smoky, and bold enough to wake your grill.

Prep: 5 min   Cook: 0 min   Yields: About ¾ cup

YOU'LL NEED

- ¼ cup finely ground coffee (dark roast)
- 2 tbsp brown sugar
- 1 tbsp smoked paprika
- 1 tbsp salt
- 1 tbsp black pepper

Five ingredients. Deep flavor. Instant steakhouse magic.

HOW TO MAKE IT

1. **Combine** all ingredients in a bowl and mix thoroughly.
2. **Pat** meat dry and coat evenly with rub before grilling or smoking.
3. **Rest** rubbed meat for 20–30 minutes before cooking to let flavors absorb.
4. **Store** in an airtight jar for up to 3 months.

☼ RUB SPECS (per tbsp)

Calories: 20 | **Protein:** 0 g | **Fat:** 0 g | **Carbs:** 5 g | **Sugar:** 3 g | **Fiber:** 0 g
Approximate values per tablespoon.

◐ Pitmaster Tip

Use coarsely ground coffee for a rugged crust on steak — or fine grind for smoother coverage on ribs or burgers.

▤ Victory Notes

How did it turn out?

....

....

Next time I'll tweak it with:

....

....

"Coffee in the morning. Coffee on the meat. Balance restored."

LEMON PEPPER SEASONING

Zesty, simple, and proof that not every hero is smoky.

Prep: 5 min   Cook: 0 min   Yields: About ¾ cup

YOU'LL NEED

- 2 tbsp lemon zest (fresh or dried)
- 3 tbsp black pepper (coarse ground)
- 2 tbsp salt
- 1 tbsp garlic powder
- 1 tbsp onion powder

Five ingredients. Sharp, sunny perfection.

HOW TO MAKE IT

1. **Mix** all ingredients in a small bowl until evenly combined.
2. **Spread** on a tray and let air-dry 1–2 hours if using fresh zest.
3. **Store** in an airtight jar for up to 2 months.
4. **Use** as a dry rub for chicken, seafood, or roasted vegetables.

☼ RUB SPECS (per tsp)

Calories: 5 | **Protein:** 0 g | **Fat:** 0 g | **Carbs:** 1 g | **Sugar:** 0 g | **Fiber:** 0 g
Approximate values per teaspoon.

◊ Pitmaster Tip

Add a pinch of cayenne or crushed chili flakes for a "lemon fire" blend that shines on grilled shrimp or salmon.

▤ Victory Notes

How did it turn out?

....

....

Next time I'll tweak it with:

....

....

"Sunshine and spice — bottled."

HONEY MUSTARD SAUCE

Sweet, tangy, and ready for anything that hits the grill.

Prep: 5 min   Cook: 0 min   Yields: About 1 cup

YOU'LL NEED

- ½ cup Dijon mustard
- ¼ cup honey
- 2 tbsp mayonnaise
- 1 tbsp lemon juice (or apple cider vinegar)
- 1 tsp black pepper

Five ingredients. Endless uses.

HOW TO MAKE IT

1. **Whisk** all ingredients in a bowl until smooth and glossy.
2. **Taste** and adjust — add more honey for sweetness or more mustard for bite.
3. **Chill** for 15–20 minutes to let flavors meld.
4. **Serve** as a dip, burger spread, or glaze brushed over grilled meats.
5. **Store** covered in the fridge for up to 1 week.

☼ SAUCE SPECS (per 2 tbsp)

Sauces & Rubs | 100

Calories: 80 | **Protein:** 0 g | **Fat:** 4 g | **Carbs:** 10 g | **Sugar:** 8 g | **Fiber:** 0 g

Approximate values per serving.

◌ Pitmaster Tip

Warm gently before brushing over chicken or ribs — it forms a beautiful golden glaze when it hits the flame.

▤ Victory Notes

How did it turn out?

....

....

Next time I'll tweak it with:

....

....

"Sweet meets heat — and balance wins."

SIMPLE TERIYAKI SAUCE

Sweet, sticky, and built to make anything shine.

Prep: 5 min   Cook: 10 min   Yields: About 1½ cups

YOU'LL NEED

- ½ cup soy sauce
- ¼ cup honey (or brown sugar)
- 2 tbsp rice vinegar (or apple cider vinegar)
- 1 tbsp minced garlic
- 1 tbsp cornstarch mixed with 2 tbsp water

Five ingredients. Infinite possibilities.

HOW TO MAKE IT

1. **Combine** soy sauce, honey, vinegar, and garlic in a saucepan over medium heat.
2. **Bring** to a gentle simmer, stirring occasionally.
3. **Whisk in** the cornstarch slurry and **cook** 2–3 minutes until thick and glossy.
4. **Cool** slightly before brushing over grilled meat, chicken, or seafood.
5. **Store** in a jar in the fridge for up to 1 week.

⚙ **SAUCE SPECS (per 2 tbsp)**

Calories: 45 | **Protein:** 1 g | **Fat:** 0 g | **Carbs:** 10 g | **Sugar:** 8 g | **Fiber:** 0 g
Approximate values per serving.

💧 **Pitmaster Tip**

Add ½ tsp grated fresh ginger for a punch of brightness — or a splash of pineapple juice for a tropical twist.

📓 **Victory Notes**

How did it turn out?

....

....

Next time I'll tweak it with:

....

....

"Shiny. Savory. Simple. The glaze that steals the spotlight."

CHIMICHURRI (HERB SAUCE)

Fresh. Fiery. The green gold of the grill.

Prep: 10 min   Cook: 0 min   Yields: About 1½ cups

YOU'LL NEED

- 1 cup parsley (finely chopped)
- ½ cup olive oil
- 3 tbsp red wine vinegar
- 3 cloves garlic, minced
- 1 tsp crushed red pepper flakes

Five ingredients. Pure flavor explosion.

HOW TO MAKE IT

1. **Combine** parsley, garlic, vinegar, and red pepper flakes in a bowl.
2. **Slowly stir in** olive oil until the mixture looks glossy and loose.
3. **Season** with salt and pepper to taste.
4. **Rest** 15 minutes before serving to let flavors blend.
5. **Drizzle** over grilled steak, chicken, fish, or veggies — or use as a marinade.

⚙ SAUCE SPECS (per 2 tbsp)

Calories: 110 | **Protein:** 0 g | **Fat:** 11 g | **Carbs:** 1 g | **Sugar:** 0 g | **Fiber:** 0 g

Approximate values per serving.

◔ Pitmaster Tip

For an extra kick, swap red wine vinegar for lime juice and toss in a pinch of cumin — the "Argentine upgrade."

🮲 Victory Notes

How did it turn out?

....

....

Next time I'll tweak it with:

....

....

"Green fire for grilled perfection."

BUFFALO WING SAUCE

The legend. The heat. The reason napkins were invented.

Prep: 5 min   Cook: 5 min   Yields: About 1½ cups

YOU'LL NEED

- ½ cup hot sauce (like Frank's RedHot)
- ½ cup unsalted butter
- 1 tbsp vinegar (white or apple cider)
- 1 tsp Worcestershire sauce
- ½ tsp garlic powder

Five ingredients. Pure attitude.

HOW TO MAKE IT

1. **Melt** butter in a small saucepan over low heat.
2. **Whisk in** hot sauce, vinegar, Worcestershire sauce, and garlic powder.
3. **Simmer** 2–3 minutes, stirring constantly, until smooth and glossy.
4. **Cool slightly** before tossing wings, shrimp, or grilled chicken.
5. **Store** leftovers in the fridge up to 1 week — reheat gently before using.

SAUCE SPECS (per 2 tbsp)

Calories: 90 | **Protein:** 0 g | **Fat:** 9 g | **Carbs:** 1 g | **Sugar:** 0 g | **Fiber:** 0 g

Approximate values per serving.

● Pitmaster Tip

Add a teaspoon of honey for sticky-sweet balance, or a splash of lime juice to brighten the heat.

▤ Victory Notes

How did it turn out?

....

....

Next time I'll tweak it with:

....

....

"If it's not dripping, you're not doing it right."

CHRISTMAS BONUS

THE 5-DAY GRILL CHALLENGE

Because New Year's resolutions taste better with smoke on them.

You've flipped, rubbed, sauced, and seared your way through a full arsenal of 5-ingredient glory. Now it's time to earn your stripes — five days, five grills, five challenges that'll make you the neighborhood legend before January hits double digits.

No fancy gear. No excuses. Just you, the flame, and your appetite.

◌ Day 1: The Smoke Test — "Own Your Signature Rub"

Pick one rub from the book — any rub — and make it *yours*.
Add one secret ingredient (cocoa, coffee, chili... surprise yourself).
Grill a small cut of beef or chicken, test the flavor, and write down your new "house rub."

Pitmaster Note: Real men trademark their taste buds.

◌ Day 2: The Sauce Throwdown — "Find Your Signature Dip"

Choose one sauce — Classic BBQ, Alabama White, or Teriyaki.
Use it three ways: glaze, dip, and burger spread.
Figure out which version gets the loudest "Damn, that's good."

Pro Tip: The best sauce isn't store-bought — it's brag-worthy.

Day 3: Fire Discipline — "Cook by Feel, Not by Timer"

No stopwatch. No app.
Grill one meal using only your instincts — sight, smell, touch, and sound.
You'll learn more from 15 minutes of focus than a dozen thermometers.

If you burn it? Congratulations. You learned flavor's edge.

Day 4: The Social Smoke — "Feed the Crew"

Invite two friends, neighbors, or that one coworker who keeps sniffing your lunch.
Serve any two dishes from the book — keep it simple, keep it fun.
BBQ is a team sport, and every great pitmaster has witnesses.

Rule: No phones at the table. Only sauce stains count as proof.

Day 5: The Resolution Grill — "New Year, New Meat"

Try something you've never grilled before — fish, lamb, shrimp, or even fruit.
Push your limits and end the challenge with a victory photo.
This is how you start a year worth remembering: with smoke in the air and pride in your hands.

Write this down: The only resolution worth keeping is **"Grill More."**

You've Earned It

If you've completed all five days, you're officially part of the *5-Ingredient Pitmasters League.*
You don't need a medal — you've got the apron scars to prove it.

Now grab a drink, look at your grill, and whisper the sacred words:

"See you next weekend, old friend."

Made in the USA
Middletown, DE
09 December 2025

24612519R00064